MAKING AND USING GRAPHS

TALLY CHARTS

by Lisa Colozza Cocca illustrated by Kathleen Petelinsek

Published in the United States of America by Cherry Lake Publishing
Ann Arbor, Michigan
www.cherrylakepublishing.com

Consultants: Janice Bradley, PhD, Mathematically Connected Communities,
New Mexico State University; Marla Conn, Read-Ability

Editorial direction: Rebecca Rowell
Book design and illustration: The Design Lab

Photo credits: Monkey Business Images/iStockphoto, 4; iStockphoto, 8, 12, 20

Library of Congress Cataloging-in-Publication Data
Cocca, Lisa Colozza, 1957–
  Tally charts / Lisa Colozza Cocca.
      pages cm. — (Making and using graphs)
  Includes index.
  ISBN 978-1-61080-916-0 (hardback : alk. paper) — ISBN 978-1-61080-941-2
(paperback : alk. paper) — ISBN 978-1-61080-966-5 (ebook) — ISBN 978-1-
61080-991-7 (hosted ebook)
1. Tallies—Juvenile literature. 2. Mathematical statistics—Graphic methods—
Juvenile literature. I. Title.

    QA276.13.C63 2013
    519.5—dc23

                        2012031090

Cherry Lake Publishing would like to acknowledge the work
of The Partnership for 21st Century Skills. Please visit
www.21stcenturyskills.org for more information.

Printed in the United States of America
Corporate Graphics Inc.
January 2013
CLFA10

Table of Contents

CHAPTER ONE

What Is a Tally Chart?

You can track players using a tally chart.

Do you have things to count? A tally chart can help. A tally chart is a simple way to **record** numbers. If you have a team of boys and girls, a tally chart can help you track how many of each there are. Or you can record how many quarters, dimes, nickels, and pennies you've saved.

You can use tally charts to track all kinds of numbers. Let's get started!

A tally chart has many parts:

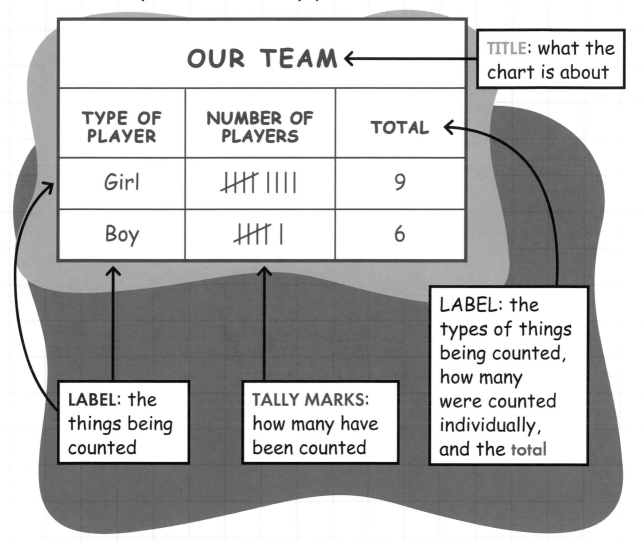

TITLE: what the chart is about

LABEL: the types of things being counted, how many were counted individually, and the total

LABEL: the things being counted

TALLY MARKS: how many have been counted

OUR TEAM		
TYPE OF PLAYER	NUMBER OF PLAYERS	TOTAL
Girl	ĤĤĤ |||||	9
Boy	ĤĤĤ		6

This tally chart has **data**, or information, about our team. The words *Girls* and *Boys* are labels. They tell us what was counted. Each kind of thing gets its own row. Are there more girls or boys on our team? How many kids are on our team?

5

We make a tally mark for each one of something we count. A tally mark is a line. We put tally marks in groups of five. This helps us count.

As we count, we draw one vertical line for each thing. Vertical lines go up and down. We draw the fifth line across the four tally marks before it.

Look at the tally marks. There are 12 of them: 5 + 5 + 2.

We make a tally mark for each thing we count.

Tally charts are an easy and helpful way to track what we count. What kinds of things can we use a tally chart to count? Let's find out!

Here's what you'll need to complete the activities in this book:

- notebook paper
- pencil with an eraser
- ruler

Gather what you need.

RULER

CHAPTER TWO

Tallying Transportation

A tally chart can help you compare the ways kids get to school.

Let's find out about our classmates. We have all kinds of differences. Kids get to school in different ways. Some take the bus, and some get a ride. Some kids walk. We can ask our classmates how they get to school and compare the numbers.

Let's make a tally chart to help us keep track of what we count.

First, we make a **table**. Next, we add labels. Then, we write down the types of transportation. They go in the Transportation **column**.

Give the chart a title.

Label the columns.

HOW WE GET TO SCHOOL

TRANSPORTATION	NUMBER COUNTED	TOTAL
Bus		
Ride		
Walk		

List the different things you want to count.

We're ready to ask our classmates how they get to school.

We make a tally mark each time we find out how a classmate gets to school. We include our own answer, too. After we have talked to each classmate, we count the tally marks in each row. We write the numbers in the right column. That's the column labeled Total.

HOW WE GET TO SCHOOL

TRANSPORTATION	NUMBER COUNTED	TOTAL
Bus	ＨＨＴ ＨＨＴ |||	13
Ride	ＨＨＴ ||||	9
Walk	ＨＨＴ		

STOP! Don't write in the book!

How many kids in our class walk to school?

We're not done yet! We need to count the marks for kids who walk. How many kids in our class walk to school?

Getting to School

Make your own tally chart about transportation.

INSTRUCTIONS:

1. Use the tally chart on page 9 as a model for your chart. If you want, use your ruler to make straight lines for the chart.
2. Ask classmates how they usually get to school.
3. Make a tally mark for each answer. Make sure you make the mark in the right row!
4. Count the tally marks in each row and write the totals in the last column.
5. Which type of transportation do most classmates use to get to school?
6. Show your classmates your chart. Tell them which type of transportation is most popular.

To get a copy of this activity, visit www.cherrylakepublishing.com/activities.

SCHOOL BUS

CHAPTER THREE

Tallying Pets

Let's find out more about our classmates. What else can we ask them? Pets! We can find out the types and number of pets they have. We'll use a tally chart to help us figure out which kind of pet is most popular.

You can track pets in a tally chart.

First, we make a table. Let's focus on dogs and cats. We give each of those its own row. Some kids might have a different kind of pet, such as a fish or a lizard. We can count those in a row labeled Other. Some kids may not have a pet. Since we're counting pets, we won't mark those answers.

Okay, we're ready to ask classmates about their pets. The first classmate we ask has a cat. We make one tally mark in that row.

OUR PETS		
PET	NUMBER	TOTAL
Dog		
Cat	I	
Other		

This row is for pets that aren't a dog or a cat.

We ask the rest of our classmates about their pets. We ask what kind and how many. We fill in our tally chart as we go. We make sure to record our own pets, too.

We put a tally mark in the chart to show each person's answers. If someone has a dog and a cat, we add two tally marks—one in each category. If a classmate has two dogs, we mark two tally marks. What comes next?

OUR PETS

PET	NUMBER	TOTAL
Dog	ЖЖ ЖЖ |||	
Cat	ЖЖ ЖЖ	
Other	ЖЖ		

STOP! Don't write in the book!

What are the totals?

Let's find our totals. We count the marks in each row. Next, we write our answers in the Total column. Our classmates have 13 dogs. How many cats do they have? How many kids have a pet that's not a dog or a cat?

Popular Pets

Practice making your own tally chart to track pets.

INSTRUCTIONS:
1. Use the tally chart on page 13 as a model for your chart. If you want, use your ruler to make straight lines for the chart.
2. Ask your friends or classmates about their pets.
3. Make a tally mark in your chart each time you get an answer. If someone has more than one pet, make a mark for each pet. Make sure you put the mark in the right row.
4. Count the tally marks in each row. Write the numbers in the Total column.
5. Which type of pet is most popular? How many pets aren't a dog or a cat?
6. Show your friends or classmates the results. Are you surprised by the results?

To get a copy of this activity, visit www.cherrylakepublishing.com/activities.

15

CHAPTER FOUR

Tallying Snacks

It's almost snack time. Let's find out which type of snack each classmate wants, so we know how many we need. There are five options. We'll count yogurt, granola bars, cheese, graham crackers, and carrot sticks. Yum! A tally chart will help us.

Let's use a tally chart to make sure we get enough of each kind of snack.

First, let's make a table for our data. We're counting five kinds of things this time, so we need a bigger tally chart.

SNACKS FOR CLASS		
SNACK	NUMBER	TOTAL
Yogurt		
Granola Bar		
Cheese		
Graham Crackers		
Carrot Sticks		

We have many snacks to choose from.

We put the names of the snacks in the Snack column. We'll make our tally marks in the middle column. It's labeled Number.

What comes next? That's right! We count the tally marks and write the amounts in the Total column.

Let's finish our tally chart.

Thanks to the tally chart, we know how many of each snack to get.

SNACKS FOR CLASS		
SNACK	NUMBER	TOTAL
Yogurt	‖‖‖ ‖‖‖	9
Granola Bar	‖‖‖ ‖	6
Cheese	‖‖‖	4
Graham Crackers	‖‖‖ ‖	6
Carrot Sticks	‖‖	3

What does our chart tell us? We need the same number of granola bars as graham crackers. How many more cheese snacks do we need than carrot sticks? Which snack do we need most of?

Snacks at Your House

It's your turn. Track snacks at your house.

INSTRUCTIONS:
1. Use the tally chart on page 17 as a model for your chart. If you want, use your ruler to make straight lines for the chart.
2. Write down some of the snacks you have in your house. Next, count how many of each snack you find.
3. Make a tally mark in the right spot for each snack you count.
4. Add up the tally marks in each row and write the totals in your chart.
5. Show your tally chart to a friend. Can your friend tell you how many apples you have?
6. Write down a few questions your friend can answer using the data in your chart.

To get a copy of this activity, visit www.cherrylakepublishing.com/activities.

CHAPTER FIVE

Tally Charts Are Fun

Tally marks are an easy way to track amounts.

Tally charts are easy to make. They're fun, too. They help us track the things we count. They help us compare amounts of things.

You compared types of transportation, pets, and snacks. What else can you count and compare with a tally chart? Practice and find out!

Here are some more fun ways you can use tally charts:

- Flip a coin 20 times. Track the number of times it lands heads up and tails up.

- Watch a basketball game. Find out how many free throws each team makes.

- Sort animal crackers. Use a tally chart to show how many you have of each animal.

- Go to the zoo. Record how many of the animals you see walk, swim, or fly.

With a tally chart, you can track coin flips, free throws, and all kinds of things. Give it a try!

Glossary

column (KAH-luhm) a line of data that goes from top to bottom

data (DAY-tuh) information recorded about people or things

label (LAY-buhl) a name; to give something a name

record (ri-KORD) to write down

row (roh) a line of data that goes from side to side

table (TAY-buhl) a square chart with rows and columns that lists data

tally mark (TAL-ee mahrk) a line that stands for one item of something being counted

title (TYE-tuhl) the name of a chart

total (TOH-tuhl) a sum; the amount after adding

For More Information

BOOKS

Harris, Trudy, and Andrew Harris. *Tally Cat Keeps Track.* Minneapolis: Millbrook, 2011.

Murphy, Stuart J. *Tally O'Malley.* New York: HarperCollins, 2004.

Nelson, Robin. *Let's Make a Tally Chart.* Minneapolis: Lerner Classroom, 2012.

WEB SITES

BrainPOP Jr.—Tally Charts and Bar Graphs
www.brainpopjr.com/math/data/tallychartsandbargraphs/
Watch a fun video about making a tally chart and using it to make a bar graph.

SoftSchools.com—Tally Chart
www.softschools.com/math/data_analysis/tally_chart/
Read a tally chart to answer the questions in this game.

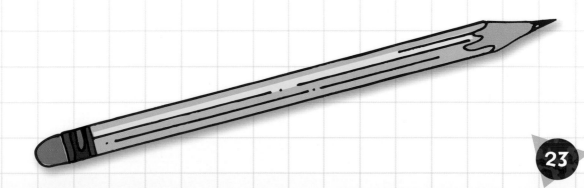

Index

About the Author

Lisa Colozza Cocca is a former teacher and school librarian. For the past decade, she has worked as a freelance writer and editor. She lives, works, and plays in New Jersey. Lisa thinks graphs are lots of fun.